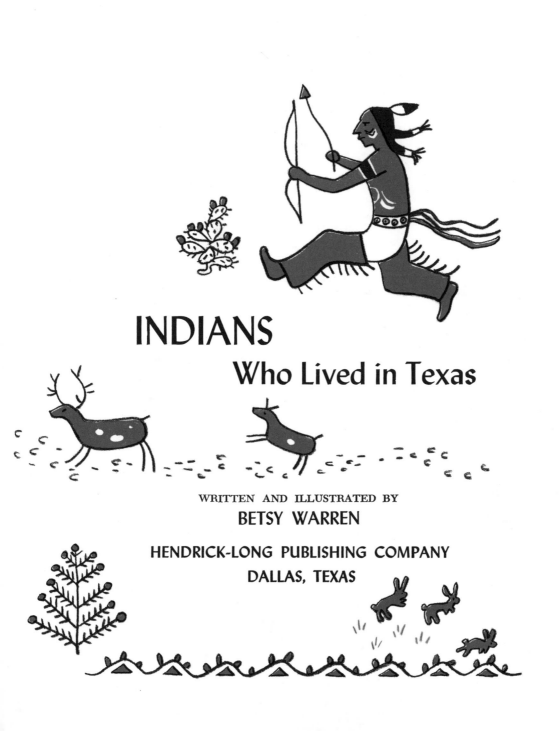

INDIANS
Who Lived in Texas

WRITTEN AND ILLUSTRATED BY
BETSY WARREN

HENDRICK-LONG PUBLISHING COMPANY
DALLAS, TEXAS

ISBN 0-937460-02-8

(Previously published by Steck-Vaughn Co. under ISBN 0-8114-7700-2)

Library of Congress Catalog Card Number 71-76607

Seventh Printing 1994

INTRODUCTION

For hundreds of years Indians were the only people who lived in the area now called Texas. They lived close to the world of nature—hunting, fishing, and gathering plants for their existence. Their habits and customs were so well adapted to outdoor life that they remained almost unchanged until the coming of the white settlers.

There were many different tribes in Texas, and they spoke many different languages. In order to communicate with each other, they developed an excellent sign language. Using their hands and fingers to picture what they wanted to say, the Texas Indians were so clearly understood, they seldom needed an interpreter.

Texas Indians did not write down stories of their history because none of the tribes had alphabets. All of them, however, used pictographs and petroglyphs to tell stories. A pictograph is a picture painted on a cave wall, a rock, or a piece of hide. A petroglyph is a picture carved with a sharp tool on rock or clay. Pictographs and petroglyphs can be found on the walls of caves and cliffs throughout Texas. These drawings give us added insight into the history of Indians who lived in Texas. They reveal the customs and religious beliefs of the people who drew them. The pictures are mainly of men, animals, and tools or of geometric designs. Only a few drawings of plants have been discovered.

3

While many of the pictures are crude and roughly executed, all are unique artistic expressions. They are like messages from the past.

From the pictographs, petroglyphs, and artifacts, from written accounts of early European explorers, and from a few surviving tribe members, we are given a fairly accurate description of the Indians who lived in Texas. Some of these tribes were peaceably settled as farmers in large villages. Others were fierce warriors who roamed over the hills and plains in search of food. Some Indians were as tall as Europeans; others were very short. But all had black hair, reddish bronze skin, and high cheekbones.

The descriptions that follow are of the ten chief tribes that inhabited Texas until the early 1900s: Caddoes (*Kah*-doz), Wichitas (*Wich*-a-taws), Jumanos (Zhu-muh-*nos*), Karankawas (Ka-*rank*-a-was), Atakapans (A-*tack*-a-puns), Tonkawas (*Tonk*-a-was), Coahuiltecans (Koa-*weel-ta*-cuns), Kiowas (*Ki*-o-was), Lipan Apache (Li-*pahn* A-*pach*-e), and Comanche (Ko-*man*-che). Only a brief mention is made of the remnants of two Indian tribes now living in Texas, the Alabama-Coushatta (Ko-*shat*-a) and Tiguas (*Te*-wuhs), since both groups immigrated to Texas from other areas.

4

The Farmers

CADDOES AND WICHITAS

The Caddo Indians built their villages in the Piney Woods area of East Texas near the Louisiana border. The Wichita clans lived north of the Caddoes near the present sites of Fort Worth and Dallas. Both the Caddoes and the Wichitas were primarily farmers, although they did hunt and fish occasionally.

Location

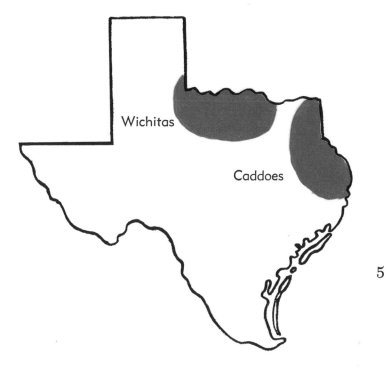

5

Appearance   All Indians of Texas, including the East Texas Indians, practiced tattooing. Using sharp-pointed rocks, thorns, and bones, both men and women scratched circles and stripes on their faces and birds and plants on their bodies. They rubbed ashes into the scratches to leave blue marks when the skin healed.

Wichitas and Caddoes painted themselves with bright colors and wore shells, bones, animal teeth, seeds, and feathers as ornaments. They pierced their ears in several places and hung ornaments from them. Caddo men also wore ornaments suspended from their noses; in fact, the name "Caddo" means "pierced nose."

6

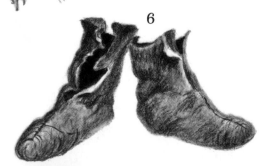

Women oiled and parted their hair in the middle, plaited it into one braid at the back, and tied a knot at the end with a rabbit or snake skin that had been dyed red. They wore sleeveless buckskin (deerskin) blouses and skirts fringed along the hem and trimmed with metal trinkets and colorful seeds. They wore fur capes in cold weather.

gourd ladle

horn spoon

mortar and pestle
used for grinding
corn

7

clay bowl

Dwellings   The Caddoes and the Wichitas built their homes in fertile fields where they could raise crops. Each village—with sometimes as many as 800 people living in it—was a cluster of grass huts that looked like beehives. Each hut had one circular room about fifteen to thirty feet in diameter with a high ceiling. Usually two families, ten to twelve persons, lived in one hut.

8

To build the framework for a hut, the workers dug fifteen to twenty holes in a circle and planted strong cedar poles in them. A single knobbed post with a crosspiece at the top was placed in the middle of the circle. Two men sat on the crosspiece and lassoed the tops of the poles, pulling them together and tying them with wet leather straps.

The walls were made by lacing and braiding the framework with saplings and grapevines. The women plastered the sides with mud and thatched the roof with bundles of straw and cornstalks. An escape hole was always left at the top for smoke from the fire that burned in the middle of the floor space. The hut had no windows and two narrow doors, one facing east, the other west.

Two other smaller huts without sides were used by families as resting, working, and storage places.

9

Food The East Texas climate was wet enough for the Caddoes and Wichitas to raise corn, beans, melons, pumpkins, tobacco, and squash. They found an abundance of wild berries, nuts, figs, peaches, and, on occasion, honey.

Corn was their favorite and most important garden crop. Each family saved enough corn for two years of planting in case fire or drouth destroyed a crop, and this seed could not be eaten even if the family were starving.

10

The farming Indians were clever hunters. **Hunting** Before horses were brought to Texas, the Indians used dogs in hunting bear, javelina, and buffalo. The dogs not only tracked down the animals, but they also carried supplies on a *travois*, a V-shaped sled made of saplings.

The Indians usually trapped such animals as the rabbit, coyote, fox, and beaver in pits that had been dug and baited.

travois

bear

jackrabbit

javelina

coyote

fox

buffalo

11

beaver

Crafts   The East Texas Indians, especially the Caddoes, are famous for their pottery. They molded jars and bowls by hand from the fine clays of East Texas. They polished their pottery with slick stones and then scratched designs on it with shells and sharp sticks.

They also split bamboo canes into threads and wove them into mats, sieves, traps, and baskets. They lined some of the baskets with clay to make water jugs. The women carried the jugs and other loads on their backs in baskets attached to headbands. These headbands which circled their foreheads were called "tumplines," and they helped to balance the weight of the load.

12

Not all of the men in a tribe were warriors—only those who chose to be. Warriors had much honor shown them. And the warriors who brought home captives, scalps, and loot became heroes of the tribe.

When an Indian decided to marry, there was no formal ceremony. The suitor left a gift of venison (deer meat) at the door of a girl's home. If her parents took the offering, the marriage was considered granted, and the groom went to live with the bride's parents. If they did not touch his offering, this was a sign that he had better find someone else for a wife.

Customs

13

Religion

Although East Texas Indians had no religious idols, they prayed to the sun, wind, thunder, and earth as symbols of power. They believed that the supreme power was a spirit called "Not-Known-to-Man" who was hidden in the sky.

The shaman, or medicine man, of the Wichitas believed that when he was in a trance, a guardian animal would give him needed instructions.

End of Culture

For a long time the Caddo and Wichita Indians of East Texas had well-developed and successful societies. However, when hunters on horseback came into their territory, they were overwhelmed because they could not get enough horses to compete with the hunters. Then the diseases carried by white European settlers spread and killed most of them, and their cultures were destroyed. They are remembered as the most advanced Indians who lived in Texas.

14

JUMANOS

Although the Jumano Indians were farmers like the East Texas Indians, they were quite different in their customs and manner of living. The difference was partly due to the climate of southwestern Texas where they lived. The area was the flat, arid, hot country near the Rio Grande and Lower Rio Conchos in the Big Bend country. Since there was little rainfall and the Jumanos did not know how to irrigate their fields, farming was a difficult task. Jumano families frequently starved.

Jumanos

15

Appearance   Jumanos were noted for cleanliness and neatness. Men cut their hair short up to the middle of their heads. The remaining hair was painted and looked like a small cap. Feathers of geese, cranes, and hawks were fastened into it. The women wore their hair loose or tied to the head.

Thread made from twisted cotton was used to weave cloth and to string copper ornaments into necklaces. Jumanos also made bands of coral and turquoise for nose and ear ornaments.

16

Jumanos lived in houses in five major settle- **Dwellings**
ments. The houses were called *pueblos*. The
pueblos were built around a central plaza. They
were made of stone or *adobe*—a mixture of ashes,
dry grass, dirt, and water that hardens and be-
comes durable when it dries in the sun.

The pueblos were low and square, and some
were two stories high. The flat roofs were so
strong that whole families could stand on them.

17

adobe brick

Food　　Since the Jumanos depended on streams and rain for their crops, they lived close to rivers. Both men and women worked in the fields. They raised fairly good crops of beans, squash, corn, and cotton. They also gathered wild plants.

The Jumanos used pottery and gourds as cooking utensils. They practiced stone boiling by heating stones in a fire, picking them up with stick tongs, and dropping them into a utensil partly filled with water. When the water started to boil from the heat of the stones, the food was added. Cooled stones were continuously replaced with hot ones until the food was done. When pottery or gourds were not available for utensils, a piece of rawhide was pressed into a hole dug in the ground to serve as a container.

Hunting   Jumano men who hunted for buffalo had to travel through the Davis Mountains to the northern plains. Before horses were used, the hunters walked these long distances. They carried hides and meat from the hunt on their backs or hauled them with dog travois. Much of the meat was dried and cut into thin strips of jerky to keep it from spoiling on the journey home.

20

The Jumanos had a strange way of greeting visitors. They did not come out of their houses to greet the visitors but prepared a special house for them. Inside they sat around the walls with their hair hanging down from bowed heads and their possessions gathered in a heap on the floor. This was their way of saying "Welcome." **Customs**

When the arid lands of the southwest could no longer yield enough food to support them, the Jumanos drifted into the mining regions of Mexico or joined the Apache hunters. There is no trace of the Jumanos today. **End of Culture**

21

The Fishermen

KARANKAWAS AND ATAKAPANS

Location

Five groups of Karankawas lived on the Gulf Coast from Galveston to Corpus Christi Bay. The Atakapans lived to the north of the Karankawas on the coast toward the lower Trinity and San Jacinto rivers. There were not many Atakapans, perhaps never more than 3500 people.

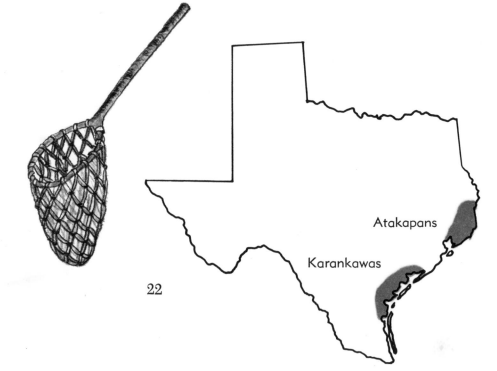

22

The tribes of Karankawas and Atakapans lived in a more primitive manner than the Caddo and Wichita farmers. Perhaps this was because they had to roam continuously along the coastal waters in order to find enough food for their families. Usually they camped less than a week in one place but returned to it each year.

They moved across the bays and lagoons in frail dugout canoes made of tree trunks cut in half and hollowed out by scraping or burning. The canoe, about fifteen inches wide and forty to fifty feet long, was long enough to hold a man, his family, and their possessions.

Appearance   The Karankawa men were tall, powerfully built people who wore pieces of cane pushed through holes made in the lower lip and on each side of the chest. The Atakapan people were short and stout. They had huge heads covered with coarse, bushy hair. Their cheekbones were especially high, and their large lips protruded over teeth stained from the various leaves which they chewed.

Men of the fishing tribes seldom wore more
than a long, fringed breechcloth and often did
not wear any clothes. In winter they wore fur
robes, but their feet were bare. Women wore
skirts of deerskin or Spanish moss tied at the
waist with thongs of rawhide. Shawls of Spanish
moss were worn over their left shoulders.

All of the tribes of fishing Indians smeared themselves with alligator grease and dirt to ward off the mosquitoes that swarmed in the marshy lands.

Head flattening was practiced by many of these coastal tribes. A thin board padded with moss and cloth was tied to a small baby's head for a year. This caused the head to slope and become somewhat pointed. It was considered a mark of beauty by these Indians.

26

Huts of the fishing tribes had to be easy to **Dwellings**
dismantle and carry. Women quickly constructed
them of willow poles. The upright poles were
pushed into the ground in a square or rounded
shape, and a framework of horizontal poles was
tied on. Skins and woven mats were thrown over
the frame, usually only on one or two sides.
These could be easily rearranged as the wind
shifted.

Atakapans often built their huts on old shell
heaps called *midden*s. The hut of the shaman
was on the highest midden.

The main part of the diet of the Karankawas **Food**
and the Atakapans was from the Gulf waters:
oysters, clams, scallops, turtles, and underwater
plants. When these were scarce, the tribes ate
locusts, lice, tallow, and bear fat. They gathered
nuts, berries, and seeds and used them in meat
stews. Prairie hens, cranes, and quail were considered delicacies.

27

Customs   Karankawas and Atakapans held ceremonial dances and festivals like other Indians of Texas. Dances were wild and noisy with much leaping and jumping around huge bonfires. Only the men danced; the women sang at some distance away from the fire. The dances often lasted three days and nights—until everyone was exhausted.

End of Culture   It is believed that no Karankawas remained in Texas after 1858. A few Atakapans were reported to be living in Texas as late as 1885.

The Plant Gatherers

TONKAWAS AND COAHUILTECANS

Tonkawas had scattered villages along the **_Location_** rivers and creeks of Central Texas. Sometimes they camped on middens. Coahuiltecans lived inland from Galveston Bay to the Rio Grande and westward to the area around present-day San Antonio. The Tonkawas and the Coahuiltecans lived in small bands, each protecting its own area and attacking outsiders who came into it. Finding enough to eat took so much time and strength that the Tonkawas and Coahuiltecans remained primitive in their habits.

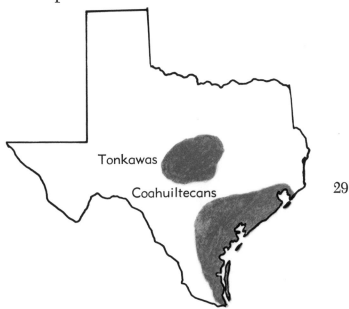

Tonkawas

Coahuiltecans

29

breechcloth

powder horn

30

Both the Tonkawas and the Coahuiltecans were small, well-built people. The men wore breechcloths which reached below their knees and were decorated with animal teeth and dried seeds. They wore long earrings and necklaces of shells, bones, and feathers. Their headdresses were elaborately decorated with animal horns and bright feathers. They parted their hair in the middle and tied beaver fur around their long braids.

Women wore short skirts made of buckskin or rabbit skins which had been twisted into strands and woven together. They parted their hair in the middle and let it hang free. Black stripes were painted over their faces and bodies.

Since the tribes of plant gatherers spent most **Dwellings** of the year looking for food, they lived in shelters which were usually little more than brush lean-tos. They were low circular huts made of willow saplings bent into a dome shape. These were covered with grass, brush, or hides.

31

Food   Pecans, acorns, and mesquite beans were the main plant foods gathered by these tribes. Herbs, roots, seeds of the sunflower, and fruits—especially the tuna of the prickly-pear cactus—were eaten when they could be found. Since buffaloes were scarce in central and southeastern Texas, the plant-gathering Indians hunted rabbits, turtles, skunks, rats, snakes, deer, and javelinas. They also ate dogs and horses and, when they could find them, fish and oysters. Even spiders, ant eggs, worms, lizards, rotten wood and other refuse were eaten. Sometimes they sweetened drinks and stews with handfuls of earth.

Raw meat was dried into paper-thin strips of jerky or pounded into *pemmican*, a kind of sausage. Fish were dried and ground into flour or cooked and left out in the open for eight days. When swarms of insects had gathered on them, they were eaten as a special treat.

pecan

acorn

mesquite
bean

sunflower

32

prickly-pear cactus

To catch deer and smaller animals, the Ton-   *Hunting*
kawas and Coahuiltecans hunted in *surrounds*.
A surround was a large circle of people—usually
women, children, and older men—who walked
slowly toward the center of the circle. This drove
the animals within the circle towards a corral
which had been made of timbers. Once inside,
the animals were killed by waiting men.

33

Customs   Among the Coahuiltecans, boys and men who died were mourned for three months by relatives. During this time the mourners could not leave the camp even to find food, but had to be fed by relatives. When food was scarce, they often starved.

Tonkawas did not name their babies until they were several years old and seldom punished them. Their method of discipline was to throw water on an offender.

End of Culture   Many of the Tonkawas and Coahuiltecans went into Mexico and joined tribes there. European invaders and their epidemics of smallpox and measles exterminated the rest of the tribes that roamed Central Texas.

34

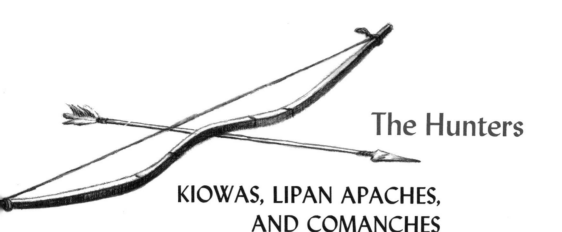

The Hunters

KIOWAS, LIPAN APACHES, AND COMANCHES

The hunting tribes of the West Texas plains were the most aggressive of all Texas Indians. The most important hunting tribes were the Kiowas, the Lipan Apaches, and the Comanches. These were proud, independent people. They were also fierce warriors who strove to control the plains where great herds of buffalo lived. They roamed constantly from the northern part of West Texas down to the border and over into Mexico and New Mexico. At one time these tribes were all enemies, but eventually they shared hunting territories.

Location

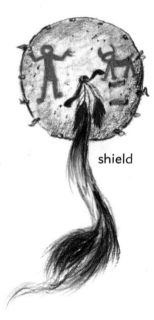

shield

Comanches

Kiowas

Lipan Apaches

knife in sheath

35

The clothes of the hunting Indians were well adapted to outdoor life. In warm weather men wore the breechcloth which was attached to a belt and hung to their knees. During cold weather leggings made of tanned buffalo or deerskin covered the body from the foot to the hip and were decorated with beads, shells, and animal teeth. They also wore shirts with V-necks that were made from the skins of deer, antelope, buffalo, or sheep. Furry buffalo robes, bisonhide boots, and even woven snowshoes were used to combat the extreme cold of the plains.

leggings

man's shirt

36

snowshoes

The Kiowa and Lipan Apache males cut their hair on the left side even with the top of the ear, possibly to show off ear ornaments. The right side of the hair was never cut. It grew almost to the ground and was tied up in a loop with a string of deer sinew.

Comanches plaited their long hair into two braids and painted the part in the middle red, yellow, or white. The braids were bound with beaver fur or cloth, and feathers were attached to the side or top of their heads.

The use of red paint distinguished Comanches from other hunting tribes. Both men and women painted their faces red. For war parties, men painted their long lances and even their horses' heads and tails red. Although red was used most frequently, yellow, blue, green, and black were also used in their designs. Each warrior painted his face as he wished with his favorite designs.

38

Women of the hunting tribes wore earrings and bracelets made of copper wire, beads or shells, and small bones. They parted their hair in the middle with one braid hanging down the back. Clam shells cut into bars were strung and worn around the neck, ankles, and wrists. Comanche women painted red and yellow lines above and below their eyes and painted circles and triangles of orange on their cheeks. Red was also smeared inside their ears.

39

Dwellings   Every spring the hunting tribes made new te-
pees of buffalo hides that had been fitted, sewn
together, and painted with designs. These hides
were thrown over a number of poles to form a
cone. Sticks of wood were used as pins to close
the sides together at the front of the tepee. At
the bottom, the hides were fastened with pegs
into the ground and could be easily rolled up in
warm weather to let the breeze in.

40

Buffalo was of the greatest importance to the Comanches, Kiowas, and Apaches. They ate every part of the animal except the skin, hooves, and bones and used these parts that they didn't eat in other ways. Unless they were starving, the hunting tribes did not eat fish, wild fowl, dogs, or coyotes. Bears were killed for their fat to be used as seasoning and grease, but seldom was the meat eaten. Stew made from pemmican mixed with berries and nuts was a favorite of the plains. Pieces of pemmican covered with honey were enjoyed as a dessert by Plains Indians. They also considered it healthful to drink the warm blood of a freshly killed animal.

nuts

berries

41

deer

wild turkey

pemmican

quail

prickly-pear cactus

Hunting   Buffalo hunting was done in the fall and spring when herds gathered on the plains in large numbers. In spring the buffalo were fat on the early grass, and in fall their hair was thicker.

When a herd was found by Indian scouts, camp was made—usually near a water hole.

Every night dances were held to insure the success of the hunt, and leaders were chosen in councils made up of all the braves. These councils decided all matters of importance to the tribe—feast times, hunts, wars, and peace treaties. The most successful warriors and hunters were chosen as leaders, and they were given much respect.

After young boys had scouted for the buffalo,
parties of hunters encircled the herd, driving
it into a small area enclosed by natural rock
"fences" or into a corral built of brush and rocks.
Bareback riders came close to the right side of
a buffalo and shot an arrow into its flank down-
ward behind the ribs. If the arrow was well
aimed, it went into the heart and killed the animal quickly. Sometimes herds were stampeded
over a cliff, and Indians waiting below would
shoot or spear animals not killed in the fall.

Eagle feathers were the most highly prized possession, for the eagle was considered the bravest of all birds. Obtaining eagle feathers was difficult since the eagle had to be caught by hand. He flew too high to be shot by bow and arrow. An Indian hunter dug a deep pit near the eagle's nesting place, hid in it, and covered himself with branches. Bait, such as a live rabbit, was tied by the pit to attract the eagle. As the bird landed to eat the bait, the hidden Indian grabbed him by the feet. Working quickly to avoid being beaten by the wings, the hunter threw the bird to the ground and stepped on its back to crush it.

The difficulty of hunting the eagle only added to the demand for its feathers. The feathers were kept clean and stored in leather bags when not being used so that they lasted for many years.

44

When a young man was ready to become a warrior, he was sent alone to a hill at a great distance from the camp. With only a pipe, a robe, tobacco, and firelighting materials, he stayed for four days and nights to await visions. The visions were to show him the direction for his life and reveal symbols to paint and songs to sing which would be his alone. No one else could use a warrior's symbols or songs unless given permission. The power given to a man through his visions was the source of his decisions throughout his life, and he was expected to pass this faith in visions on to others.

Customs

The wars and diseases of the white man came to the Kiowas, Lipan Apaches, and Comanches. By the early 1900s there were virtually none of them left in Texas.

End of Culture

CONTRIBUTIONS

When the white man came to Texas, he learned
many things from the Indians that helped him to
live on the frontier and develop the state. Geo-
graphic names remain as evidence of our rich
Indian heritage—names of rivers, counties, cities.
Even the name *Texas* is a legacy.

INDIANS TODAY

There are two Indian reservations in Texas
today. The largest is the Alabama-Coushatta
reservation seventeen miles from Livingston; the
reservation for the Tiguas Indians is located in
El Paso County. The Alabama and Coushatta
tribes migrated to Texas after the white man ex-
plored and settled along the Mississippi River.
The Tiguas came to Texas from New Mexico.

ILLUSTRATED GLOSSARY

breechcloth

javelina   (hav-a-**leen**-ah)

midden   (**mid**-n)

pemmican   (**pemm**-uh-cun)

petroglyph   (**pe-tro**-glif)

pictograph   (**pic-to**-graf)

prickly-pear cactus

Spanish moss

travois   (tra-**voy**)

tumpline

INDEX

DATE DUE

DATE DUE	BORROWER'S NAME	REGIS-TRAR
FEB 5 1979		25
MAR 2 7 1979	gromeo	28
SEP 1 3 1979	Nina Petrinotz	42
NOV 1 4 1980	Wilson	42